Rock Climbing and Rappeling

Paul Mason

Smart Apple Media

Smart Apple Media
2140 Howard Drive West
North Mankato, Minnesota 56003

First published in 2007 by
MACMILLAN EDUCATION AUSTRALIA PTY LTD
627 Chapel Street, South Yarra, Australia 3141

Visit our Web site at www.macmillan.com.au or go directly to www.macmillanlibrary.com.au

Associated companies and representatives throughout the world.

Library of Congress Cataloging-in-Publication Data

Mason, Paul, 1967-
    Rock climbing and rappeling / by Paul Mason.
    p. cm. — (Recreational sports)
    Includes index.
    ISBN 978-1-59920-132-0
    1. Rock climbing—Juvenile literature. 2. Rappelling—Juvenile literature. I. Title.

    GV200.2.M37 2007
    796.522'3—dc22

                                                        2007004598

Edited by Vanessa Lanaway
Text and cover design by Pier Vido
Page layout by Pier Vido
Photo research by Naomi Parker
Illustrations by Boris Silvestri
Map on pp. 28–9 by Pier Vido

Printed in U.S.

Acknowledgements
The author and the publisher are grateful to the following for permission to reproduce
copyright material:

Front cover photograph: Climber negotiating a rock, courtesy of Leeuwtje/Istockphoto.

Photos courtesy of:
Jack Ambrose/Getty Images, p. 22; Alistair Berg/VCL/Getty Images, p. 20; Hermann Erber/Getty
Images, p. 30; Zigy Kaluzny/Getty Images, p. 7; Corey Rich/Getty Images, p. 16; Philip & Karen
Smith/Getty Images, p. 4; John Terence Turner/Getty Images, p. 21; Istockphoto, p. 27;
Steven Dern/Istockphoto, p. 6; Gary Dyson/Istockphoto, p. 14; Peter Evans/Istockphoto,
p. 5; Glenn Frank/Istockphoto, p. 12 (both); Peter Galbraith/Istockphoto, p. 9; Craig Jones/
Istockphoto, p. 13 (left); Aaron Kohr/Istockphoto, p. 13 (right); Leeuwtje/Istockphoto, pp. 1, 8;
Dimitrije Ostojic/Istockphoto, p. 10; Sierrarat/Istockphoto, p. 18; Mike Tittel/Photolibrary, p. 19;
Webber Wendell/Photolibrary, p. 26; PhotoDisc, p. 11.

Please note
At the time of printing, the Internet addresses appearing in this book were correct. However,
because of the dynamic nature of the Internet, we cannot guarantee that all Web addresses
will remain correct.

Contents

Glossary words
When a word is printed in **bold**, you can look up
its meaning in the glossary on page 31.

Recreational sports

Recreational sports are the activities we do in our spare time. These are sports that people do for fun, not necessarily for competition.

You have probably tried some recreational sports already. Maybe you would like to know more about them or find out about new ones? Try as many as you can—not just climbing. Also try biking, hiking, fishing, kayaking, and snorkeling. This will help you find one you really love doing.

Benefits of sports

Recreational sports give people lots of pleasure, but they also have other benefits. People who exercise regularly usually have better health. They find it easier to concentrate and do better in school or at work.

One of the rewards of climbing up a long way is the fantastic views!

Climbing

Climbing is a great recreational sport. You can do it at almost any age, from 7 to 70 years old. There are climbs for people of all abilities. You might start on an easy 16–foot (5–m) climb at your local climbing wall. In a few years you could be hundreds of feet up.

Climbing is great exercise, helping you stay fit and healthy. Climbers depend on each other for safety and survival. Climbing is also a great way to make friends.

Climbing is a great way to get exercise and explore new places.

Getting started

There are lots of places to try climbing. Your first climb might be at a purpose-built **climbing wall**. Later, you might try climbing on natural rock.

Climbing walls

Climbing walls are a great place to try climbing. Many have special sessions for beginners. They provide all of the equipment. An instructor shows you what to do and makes sure everything is safe before you climb.

On a climbing wall, people climb using **handholds** and **footholds** bolted to the wall. Sometimes the wall is shaped like a rock.

"The best climber in the world is the one who's having the most fun."

Famous climber Alex Lowe.

Indoor climbing walls are a good place to practice rock climbing before trying natural rock walls.

Top rope climbing

People use top ropes to make sure that they do not get hurt if they fall. You will use top ropes on your first high-level climb. Top rope climbing is when you are attached to a rope that stretches above you through a metal loop and back to the ground. The metal loop is the **anchor point**. Your climbing instructor holds the other end of the rope. As you climb, your instructor pulls the rope so that it never has any **slack** in it. This is called belaying. If you slip, the top rope keeps you from falling.

Harness

Climber

Rope is pulled in

Rope

Climber goes up

Holds

Top rope climbing is a safe way to learn to climb.

Top rope climbing and belaying

These climbers will work as a team, taking it in turns to climb

Climbers usually work in teams of two. One person is the climber and the other is the belayer. The belayer uses the rope to keep the climber safe.

Rope control

Rope control means controlling how tight or loose the rope is. This is a very important skill. If the rope has too much slack in it, a fall could cause injury. If the rope is too tight, it can make it difficult for the climber to move easily.

Both the climber and belayer must work together to have good rope control.

- The belayer must carefully watch the climber, pulling in enough rope to take up any slack.
- The climber must make sure they do not climb too quickly. If they climb too fast, the belayer may not be able to pull the rope in fast enough, and there will be too much slack.

Belaying

Belaying well is just as important as climbing well. If you cannot belay safely, your climbing partner could be injured in a fall. Belayers use a belay device to pull the rope or grip it tightly. The climbing rope passes through the belay device that is attached to the climber's harness. When you are belaying:

- pay close attention to the climber
- pull in just enough rope so that it is loose, but has no extra slack
- pull through as much rope as possible if you think the climber might fall

Top tip!

When belaying, never stand far away from the base of the climb. If your partner falls, you will be pulled toward the climb by the rope.

This type of belay device is called a figure-8.

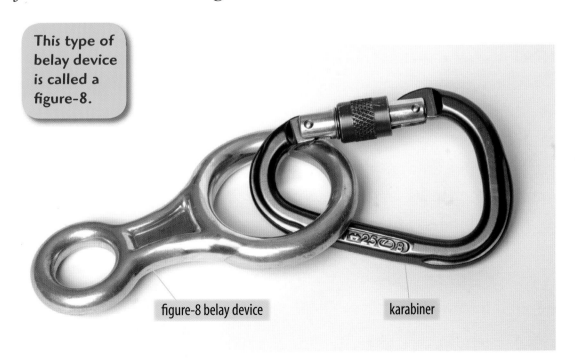

figure-8 belay device   karabiner

Climbing equipment

If you try climbing and decide you want to do more, you will need some equipment of your own.

Basic equipment

The basic equipment for climbing is very simple and fairly inexpensive. You will need:

- a pair of climbing shoes that has soft, sticky rubber soles to grip the footholds.
- a climbing harness
- an oblong piece of metal called a karabiner that has a gate that can be opened and closed or screwed shut. Karabiners are useful for attaching one thing to another.
- a belay device
- a helmet

Top rope climbers also need a rope, two or three **slings**, and three or four extra karabiners. The cost of these can quickly add up. You could share them with a group of friends, so no one needs o spend too much money.

The right climbing equipment is important for a safe climb.

WATCH OUT!

Always check that your clothes cannot get caught in the equipment while you are belaying someone.

Advanced equipment

Experienced climbers carry extra equipment attached to their climbing harness, including runners. A runner is a nylon tape with a karabiner at each end. Runners can be used to anchor the climber or the rope to the rock.

Clothing

The only rule about clothing for climbing is that it should not make it hard to stretch your body. Some climbers prefer loose clothes. Other climbers like to wear tight, stretchy clothes that cannot get caught in their climbing gear.

The right clothing should make it easy to move and stretch your body.

runners

"John Wayne never wore Lycra."
Famous American climber Ron Kauk explains why he climbs in denim jeans.

Basic technique

This climber is using a lot of energy from her arms.

By balancing on her toes, she is much more comfortable.

Most of the techniques new climbers learn will help them save energy. Climbing can be very tiring, and running out of energy halfway up a climb is a terrible feeling.

Saving energy

Experienced climbers suggest several techniques to help you save energy while climbing:

- Use your legs. Put as much weight as possible onto your feet and legs. They are stronger than your arms.
- Keep your toes forward. Put your toes on the footholds, not the inner edges of your feet. This helps take weight off your arms.
- Take small steps and make small movements. Reaching as high as you can and then pulling yourself up is very tiring.
- Plan your rests. Try to spot places on the climb where you could have a rest. Climb between them safely, but quickly.

Body position

Keeping your body in the right position will help you climb better. Many beginners keep their arms bent and their chest close to the wall. They look as if they are hugging the wall. This puts a lot of weight on their arms, and is hard work.

Tuck in your bottom, instead of sticking it out. Straighten your arms so that your chest is away from the wall. This helps your legs take your weight, instead of your arms.

"If you don't let go, you can't fall off!"

Climber Jerry Moffat explains why it is a good idea for a climber to have a strong grip!

Top tip!

If your arms get tired, give your hands a shake. It will help you relax.

This climber is taking a big step that will drain energy from her legs.

These climbers are taking smaller steps that are much less tiring.

13

Natural rock

After getting some experience on an artificial climbing wall, most climbers want to try climbing on natural rock.

Differences from artificial walls

Climbing on real rock is very different from climbing on an artificial wall. The differences are:

- Different rocks have different levels of grip. Rocks may be more slippery than an artificial wall.
- Anchor points for a top rope may not be as safe as they seem. Small trees can break or be uprooted.
- The rock can break off unexpectedly, leaving you without a handhold or foothold.

For all these reasons, never climb with another inexperienced climber. Make sure you climb on natural rock with someone who has years of experience.

When climbing on natural rock, it is important to have experienced climbers with you for safety.

Safety first

Make sure that your climb is as safe as possible. Check that the top rope is securely anchored, and that your belayer is in a good position to hold your weight.

Technique

Climbing safely

Use these tips to make sure you climb as safely as possible.

1 Attach your top rope to at least two anchor points, and make sure that the rope does not rub against the rock. This could damage it.

2 Never rappel, or slide, down a top rope right away. Always walk to the bottom, then test the rope by putting all your weight on it from the ground.

3 Always test your handhold or foothold by putting a little weight on it first. If it wobbles or creaks, there is a danger it could break off.

Bouldering

Bouldering is climbing at a very low height, usually less than head height. It is a great way to develop your climbing skills safely.

Bouldering equipment

Most climbers only use climbing shoes for bouldering. They do not need a harness or rope, because they are climbing almost at ground level.

Many climbers also use a chalk bag. This is a little bag filled with chalk dust, tied around your waist and behind you. When your fingers get slippery with sweat, you reach back and rub your fingertips in the chalk dust. This dries up the sweat and allows you to grip holds easily.

Top tip!

Watch other climbers do a bouldering move before trying it yourself.

Many climbers use chalk to give them extra grip.

Spotters

A spotter is a person who stands behind someone who is bouldering. If the climber slips off, the spotter catches them to make sure they do not fall awkwardly. A spotter should never let the climber fall on them. The idea is to try to catch the climber under the armpits, to stop them from hitting the ground at full speed.

Spotters also often give helpful advice about the climber's next move. This is especially true if the spotter has already done the move, and the climber is finding it difficult.

"The ground is a harsh spotter."

A U.S. climber.

WATCH OUT!

Never stand right below someone who is bouldering, in case they fall off.

A spotter protects the climber from hurting themselves if they fall.

Leading climbs

Climbing without a top rope is called leading. Many climbers start to climb without a top rope once they are used to climbing on real rock.

Leader and second

The two climbers on a leading climb are called the leader and the second. The leader is usually the most experienced, best climber. Their job is the most difficult and dangerous. The leader climbs first, finding the way up the climb and trailing a rope behind them.

Once the leader has reached the top, the second climbs up. Being a second is easier and safer than leading. If you slip, the leader will have a grip on the rope and can stop you from falling.

Short climbs like this are ideal for practicing leading climbs.

Leader

Second

WATCH OUT!
Helmets are especially useful for seconds, in case the leader knocks off rocks that fall on them.

If this climber slips, the rope clipped to the protection will stop him from falling clear.

Protection

Protection is the equipment that links the rope to the rock at regular intervals. Protection keeps the leader from hitting the ground if they fall. If the leader falls, the protection acts like the anchor point on a top roped climb.

When the second climbs up, they remove the protection and clip it to their harness.

Kinds of protection

There are many kinds of protection that anchor the rope to the rock. There are:

- tiny metal wedges called wires
- big bits of metal called chocks
- clever mechanical devices called cams
- purpose-built bolts, which are permanently drilled into the rock

Climbers use karabiners to attach these anchors to their ropes.

Climbing signals

Climbers on lead routes work together as a team.
They cannot always see each other, so they use special signals
to let each other know what is happening.

This second is
following the
leader up a
climb.

Climbing calls

The leader and the second
spend a lot of time talking
to each other while one of
them is climbing. These are
some of the calls they use.

"On belay?"

Climbers ask this question
to check whether their
climbing partner has
control of the rope, and
could use it to stop them
from falling. Some climbers
shout, "Ready to climb?"

"Off belay!"

This tells your climbing
partner that you are safe,
and do not need them to
carry on belaying. Some
climbers shout "Safe!"

"Slack!"

This tells the belayer that the rope is pulling you off balance. The belayer needs to **pay** a little more out.

"Climbing!"

The second shouts this to warn the leader that they are about to start following up the route. If everything is safe, the leader shouts back, "OK!" If not, they shout "Not safe!"

"Take in!"

This tells the belayer to pull in as much rope as possible. It often means the climber is worried about falling off.

Top tip!

Some climbers figure out a system of tugs on the rope in case they cannot hear each other. One tug means "On belay", and two means "Off belay."

The second hands runners back to the leader so she can start climbing ahead.

Rappeling

Rappeling is sliding down a rope in a safe, controlled way. Rappelers use a belay device to control their speed as they slide down the rope.

Rappeling safely

The safest way to rappel is with an experienced climber or instructor. However, you should still check for yourself that it is safe. Ask yourself the following questions.

- Are the anchor points completely secure?
- Is the rope in good condition and safely attached to the anchors?
- Is your harness buckled tightly shut?
- Is the belay device securely attached to your harness?

If the answer to any of these questions is "no," or if you have any doubts, DO NOT RAPPEL!

When rappeling, keep your body angled out at about 70 degrees from the rock.

How rappeling works

Rappeling works through friction. Friction occurs when two objects rub against each other. It makes them move more slowly. In rappeling, the friction comes from the rope rubbing against the belay device.

Rappelers control their speed by controlling the amount of friction between the rope and the belay device. They do this by holding the rope in different positions.

Sliding down the rope faster

Moving the loose, downhill part of the rope forward at a 90-degree angle to the belay device allows the rope to slide through faster.

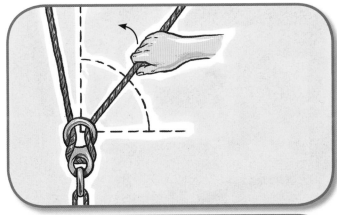

Slowing down

Pulling the rope back toward the 90-degree angle slows the speed that the rope slides through.

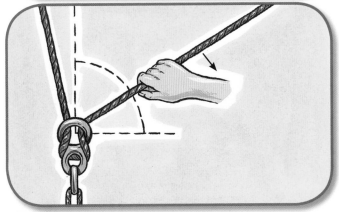

Stopping

Pulling the rope back past the 90-degree angle keeps the rope from sliding through the belay device. The rappeler can stop completely and dangle on the rope.

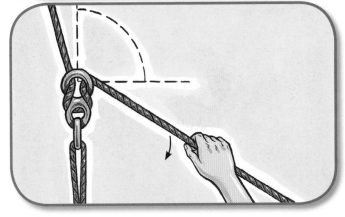

Climbing knots

Learning to tie two or three simple knots is useful for any climber. Some climbers even get through their whole climbing career using just the figure-of-eight knot.

End-of-rope knots

Climbers often have to tie a loop at the end of their rope. They use this to attach the rope to a harness or an anchor point.

Technique

Figure-of-eight knot

The figure-of-eight knot is especially useful when you have to tie the end of a rope around or through something, such as your climbing harness.

1 Hold the rope with about 6 feet (2 m) spare at the end. Turn it back on itself and over, creating a loop.	**2** Tuck the rope under itself, then pass it down through the loop. Do not pull the knot tight.	**3** Pass the end through whatever it is being tied to. Then, tuck the rope back through the knot, following the rope's path in reverse.	**4** Pull the knot tight.

Loop knots

Loop knots are used to make a fixed loop on the rope. This can then be used to attach the rope to an anchor point.

Double figure-of-eight knot

The double figure-of-eight knot can be used to make a loop in the middle of a rope. It is tied in the same way as the first half of a single figure-of-eight, but with a doubled piece of rope.

WATCH OUT!
Always pull hard on your knot to test its strength before climbing with it.

Technique

Alpine butterfly knot

The Alpine butterfly is a very strong knot, and a good alternative to the figure-of-eight loop.

1 Give the rope two twists, to make an "8" shape from two loops. The top loop should be the biggest.

2 Drop the top loop down and under the rope.

3 Pull it up through the bottom loop on the other side. Pull the knot tight. You have tied the Alpine butterfly knot.

Fit to climb

If you do some extra training, you will find it much easier to climb. General fitness is useful, but most climbers train to build specific muscles, too.

General fitness

You can build good general fitness with activities such as running, swimming, and cycling. However, climbers are careful not to build up big, heavy muscles. Most climbers are slim and light.

Simple, healthy food such as fish and salad is popular with many climbers.

Watch your weight

Most climbers are very careful not to get too heavy. After all, it is much harder to haul 150 pounds (68 kg) up a steep route than 120 pounds (54 kg). Foods such as fresh fruit and vegetables, rice, and pasta are good. Smart climbers usually do not eat fattening foods such as fries, burgers, or sweets.

"Maybe sticking to a diet is easier than climbing big walls."

A female Italian climber, halfway up the 4-day, 2950-foot (899-m) climb "Salathé Wall" in Yosemite National Park

Specialist training

Specialist training for climbers is usually designed for getting stronger fingers, hands, arms, and shoulders. These are the things that climbers use for holding on and pulling themselves up. Most people's legs are strong enough for climbing already.

One of the most popular training devices is a finger board. This is a board covered in small handholds. It is screwed to a wall just above head height. Climbers use finger boards to do pull-ups.

Balance and flexibility

Climbers need good balance, as well as strength. Some climbers practice yoga as a way of improving their balance. Yoga also makes people more **flexible**

WATCH OUT!
Never train if you have sore joints. You could make an injury worse.

Yoga helps climbers improve their flexibility, so they can reach holds more easily.

Climbing and rappeling around the world

There are famous climbing areas all around the world. The ones on this page are some of the most popular.

High risk
Name Eigerwand
Country Switzerland
Famous for One of the most dangerous climbs in the world. Over 60 people have died on the Eigerwand's north face.

For beginners and experts
Name Chamonix
Country France
Famous for Climbing routes for anyone, from beginners to the best in the world.

Moroccan mountains
Name Tafroute Valley
Country Morocco
Famous for One of the world's newly discovered rock-climbing areas, in the beautiful surroundings of North Africa's Anti-Atlas mountains.

Best climbs on Earth
Name The Restaurant
Country South Africa
Famous for Said to have some of the best climbing in the universe. More than 500 routes, and lots of unclimbed rock faces.

Test your stamina
Name   Yosemite
Country   United States
Famous for   Long "Big Wall" climbs that take several days to finish. The most famous is El Capitan, which climbers call "El Cap."

Stunning scenery
Name   Joshua Tree
Country   United States
Famous for   Amazing variety of climbs in the stunning surroundings of the Joshua Tree National Park, California.

Bouldering challenges
Name   The Grampians
Country   Australia
Famous for   Extremely tricky bouldering challenges, including the world's hardest.

Something for everyone
Name   Hanging Rock
Country   New Zealand
Famous for   At least 90 routes of varying grades to suit almost any climber.

Climbing crazy!

Robyn has been climbing since she was 11 years old. She now works as a climbing guide.

How did you first get into climbing?

My godfather took me and my brothers on a trip to the Blue Mountains, in Australia. He fixed up a top rope, and we spent a whole day going up and down about three different routes. I scraped my knees and got really tired, but I loved it so much I kept pestering him to take me again!

What are your favorite climbing places?

I still really love climbing in the Blue Mountains. I went to Europe one summer and climbed around Chamonix, which was great. But the most amazing place for any climber is Yosemite National Park.

What is your worst-ever climbing experience?

Watching someone fall from the very top of a rappeling route. They hadn't done their harness up properly, and as soon as the weight came onto it, it came undone. Fortunately, they survived.

What advice would you give to young climbers?

Just to enjoy your climbing. Don't worry about what grades other people climb at. Concentrate on your own skills and try to do each climb a little better than you did it last time. And always stay safe!

What are your favorite places for finding out about climbing?

For places in the United States, www.usaclimbing.org is a good place to find out about climbing. I also really like reading climbing guidebooks from all round the world. You can usually find than in climbing equipment shops.

Glossary

anchor point

a solid place to which a rope can be fixed

climbing wall

a wall built like a rock wall for people to practice climbing on

flexible

able to twist and bend your body easily, without straining any muscles

footholds

places where a climber's foot is able to grip

handholds

places where a climber's hand is able to grip

karabiner

an oblong piece of metal with a gate in it. The gate can be opened and closed, and on some karabiners the gate can be screwed shut. Karabiners are useful for attaching things to one another.

pay

to feed out rope

slack

the "looseness" of a climbing rope. All climbers need a little slack in their rope to allow them freedom to move, but too much slack makes climbing dangerous.

slings

strips of strong fabric tape that have been sewn or knotted into a loop, used to connect either the climber or the rope to the rock

Index